"A Dummy for Christmas"

Second Edition

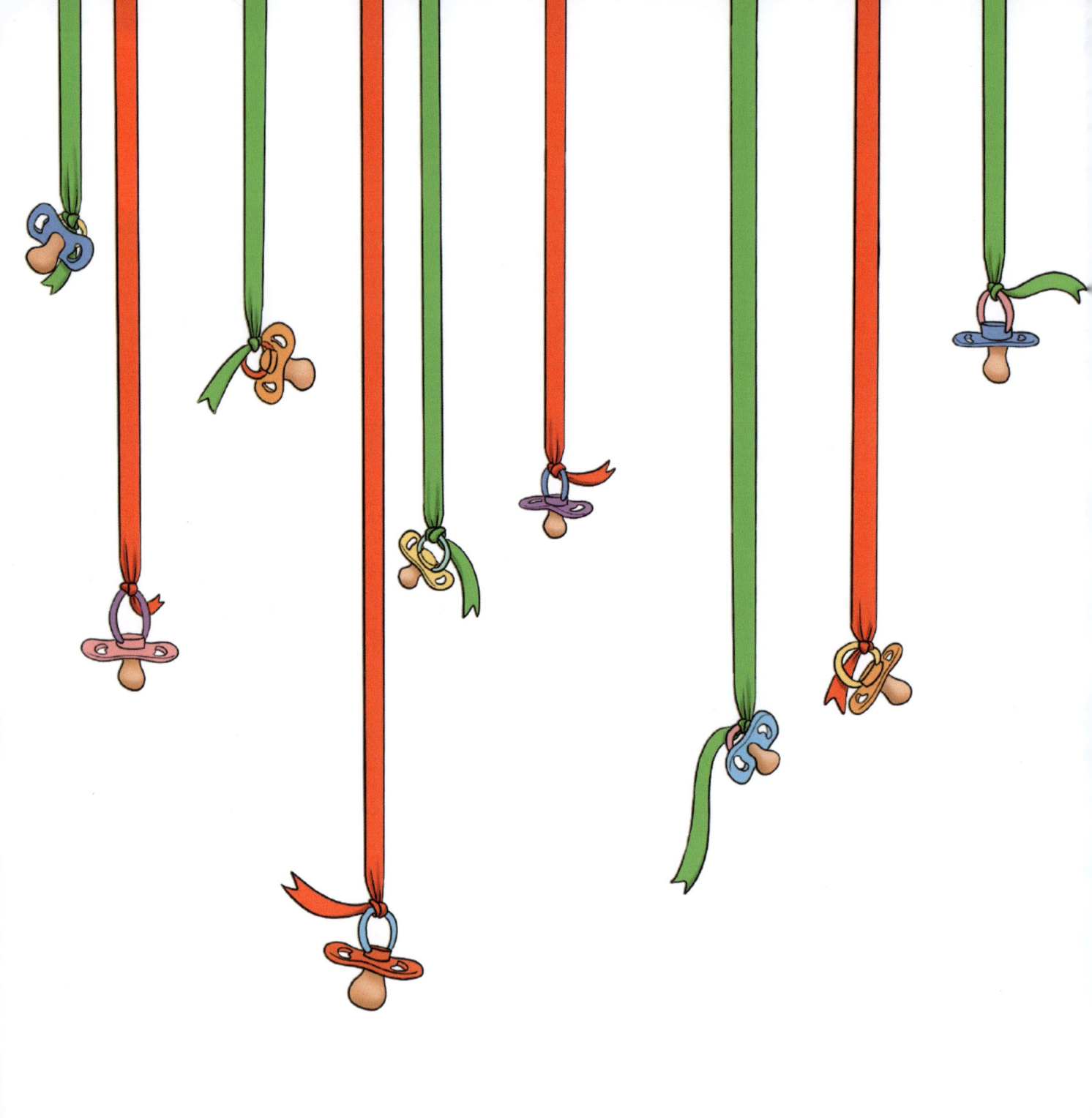

In the cold North Pole,
Where Santa calls home,
It's so quiet and peaceful,
You'd think you were alone.

But hidden in the mountains,
Upon a snowy shelf,
You'll hear the sound of toys,
Being made by an elf.

But this Christmas Eve,
Brought something very curious.
It was the sound of crying,
And Santa seemed furious.

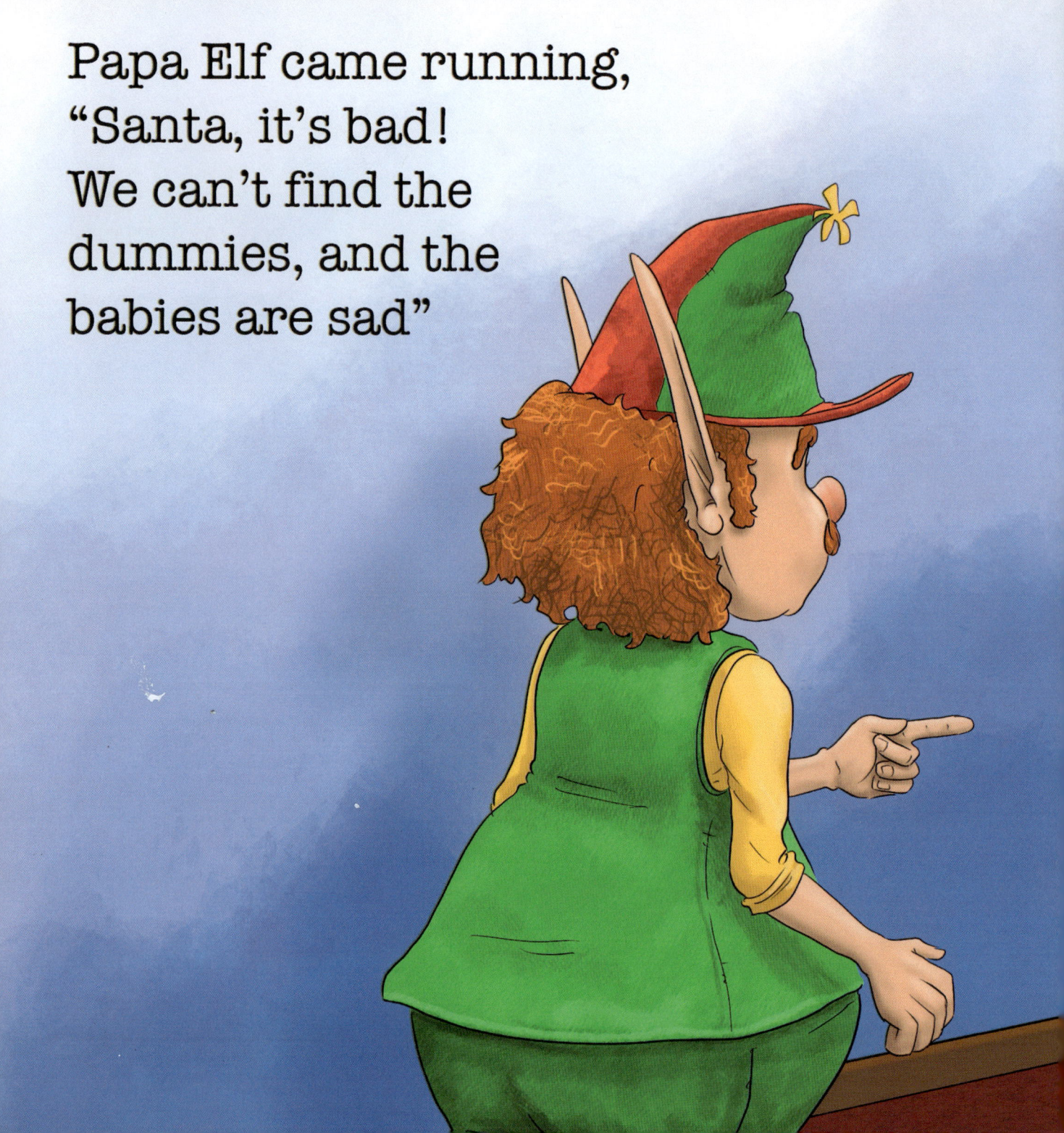

Papa Elf came running, "Santa, it's bad! We can't find the dummies, and the babies are sad"

He called every elf. The elves sons and daughters, and told them to rush, to Santa's headquarters.

Santa went fast, and packed up his sled,
He sent the children a letter,
And this is what
It said...

The elf babies need us,
they are ever so blue.
They need your help,
and I do too!

You need to look around,
and collect every dummy.
Give them to your daddy,
your granny or mummy.

The children rushed to look,
In every corner of their bed.

There was one in the kitchen,
even one in the shed.

They gathered them together,
Put them all in a jar.
Placed them under the tree,
Santa wouldn't have to look far.

Santa flew around every street, road and crescent. Collecting the dummies and leaving presents.

Then back to the North Pole, where they needed his stash.
The reindeer went quickly, as quick as a flash.

He gave them the dummies,
which he said they could keep,
and all the baby elves
went straight to sleep.

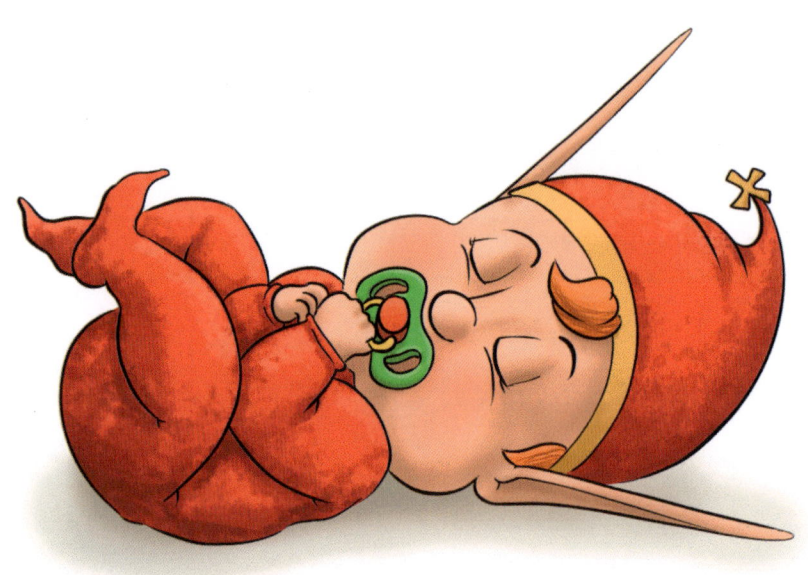

Printed in Great Britain
by Amazon